Decision Making i

Fourmat Publishing

Decision Making in Magistrates' Courts

by
Kerry Barker, LL.B, Barrister, Clerk to the
South East Hampshire Justices
and
John Sturges JP, Chairman of the
Portsmouth Bench

Foreword by His Honour
Judge Keith Devlin
Vice Chairman, Legal Committee of the
Magistrates' Association

Kerry Barker is also Clerk to the Magistrates'
Courts Committee and Joint Magistrates Training
Officer; and John Sturges is Chairman of the
Training of Magistrates Committee for Hampshire.

London
Fourmat Publishing
1986

ISBN 1 85190 017 9

First published October 1986

© Fourmat Publishing
27 & 28 St Albans Place, Islington Green,
London N1 ONX
Printed in England by
Billing & Sons Limited, Worcester

Foreword

by His Honour Judge Keith Devlin

In recent years, the work of the magistracy has become more and more complex and onerous as its jurisdiction in both civil and criminal matters has widened. Although lay justices have a professionally qualified clerk to advise them on matters of law, on the sometimes difficult areas of mixed fact and law, and on sentencing, the decisions that magistrates themselves have to make in the assessment of evidence at all the stages of the trial process and in the disposal of the case, have become increasingly demanding both in themselves and in the circumstances in which they have to be made, including the pressure of work as courts become ever more busy. In fact, the job of being a lay magistrate has never been harder.

New magistrates coming to this work for the first time will have a good idea of what magistrates do but much less of how they do it. Basic training (and later more advanced and specialist training) is, therefore, likely to be of the greatest importance and nowadays, considerable emphasis is rightly placed upon it in relation to the experience that magistrates soon acquire in sitting with their more senior colleagues — the training on the job for which there can never be any effective substitute.

This book is an important contribution to that training and a valuable aid in the evaluation of that experience — not only, I suggest, for new magistrates but also for those more senior justices who feel the need for some kind of basic refresher course. It is also likely to be especially useful for those who take the chair and therefore seek to bring a structure to the decision taking process in which their colleagues need fully to be involved. In meeting these different requirements, the book provides a lucid, step by step guide to the elements of what the authors have identified as the six key decisions which justices regularly encounter in their work in court, ie the assessment of evidence required to reach a verdict, the sentencing decision, the submission of no case, applications for adjournment, and decisions on bail and the appropriate mode of trial. Each analysis contains a check list and there are useful and illuminating case studies. There are also helpful chapters on the role of the chairman and the clerk in the decision taking process in court and in the retiring room.

The authors combine a long experience of many years on the bench as a chairman and the legal knowledge and professional expertise of a clerk to the justices. The result of this partnership is a readable, practical and non-technical book which all of us who have to make the kind of decisions it covers (or advise others to make) may read with considerable profit.

Keith Devlin
August 1986

Preface

Lay magistrates are busy people occupied with many things but voluntarily they set aside a day or half day regularly to sit in court and hear cases. Because they are lay magistrates, untrained in the law, they receive guidance from many sources. On matters of law they receive advice from their court clerks as well as listen to both prosecuting and defending advocates. Sentencing is another area in which they receive guidance. The Clerk to the Justices, through his court clerks, can provide a great deal of advice in this field. Reports from doctors or psychiatrists are sometimes thought valuable and the social enquiry reports provided by probation officers and social workers are an acknowledged aid to the sentencing process. Also, from time to time authoritative studies are published designed to assist sentencers.

Some years ago the Magistrates' Association published its "Suggestions for Traffic Offence Penalties" and this has been almost universally accepted by benches throughout the country. It came about because of the considerable public concern for consistency in sentencing. While there had been general agreement that consistency of approach was desirable, there had been little attempt to express this in terms of actual sentences. However, in spite of arguments that this was an obtrusion into the discretion exercised by individual magistrates the Association's guidelines were welcomed and were widely accepted as valuable.

Sentencing is only one of the areas in which lay magistrates have to make decisions. They are judges of fact and of law and, taking advice from such sources as are available to them, lay justices have to make decisions in virtually every conceivable aspect of a case and the way it is conducted before them. To take criminal cases as an example, magistrates' courts in England and Wales dealt with over 2.2m defendants in 1984. Involved in each of those cases, leading to each concluding decision, there was a myriad of subordinate decisions to be made.

Strangely, however, whilst lay magistrates now have available to them a great deal of guidance about such important aspects of their work as the conduct of court proceedings, making sentencing decisions and making pronouncements in court, there appears to be no widely available advice on the actual process of making decisions in judicial proceedings. Yet judicial decision making is far from easy. It does not come naturally to the majority of people and is well outside the experience of most new-comers to the Bench. After several years of studying and taking part in the process and then lecturing others about it we decided that we should attempt to fill this important void.

We hope that this guide will not be seen as another of the sentencing or speaking parts type. It does not attempt to elucidate points of law, or to draw attention to the decisions of higher courts. Nor does it attempt to enunciate sentencing principles or to suggest appropriate sentences for particular offences. There are many such valuable guides, some by academic lawyers, others by experienced practitioners, and there is no need to add to their number. This guide is altogether different. Firstly, it is written primarily for magistrates and not for legal advisers. Secondly, it is concerned with the way decisions are reached and not with the actual decisions themselves.

The techniques of decision making have long been a part of management training and there are many valuable academic studies in the field of public and industrial administration. This guide attempts to analyse the process by which lay magistrates reach their decisions. It identifies that stage when, having received all the advice from those entitled to give it, they exercise the discretion unique to their office. It examines how decisions are reached and considers the appropriate method by which that can be done. It puts forward a certain technique and makes specific suggestions.

In order to do this we have drawn upon the experience of

magistrates throughout the country. In the course of hearing cases magistrates do arrive at decisions and many will have devised their own techniques. In some cases they have worked out a method and have persuaded their colleagues to adopt it. In many cases the method will be *ad hoc*, dependent upon the members who constitute the bench. What this guide attempts to do is to codify existing practice. It takes ways which have been worked out and found to be effective by experienced magistrates — lay and stipendiary — and it builds them into a set of structures which together constitute clear guidance as to how lay magistrates can reach the various decisions which constantly confront them when dealing with cases. It is, therefore, a codification of existing practices put forward as a guide which we hope lay magistrates will find valuable. We also hope that an understanding of the process of decision making in magistrates' courts will assist advocates and all those who work in court and are responsible for presenting cases, argument or advice to lay magistrates.

Included in the guide is a theoretical justification of this approach based upon the nature of the decision making process in magistrates' courts. However, the main emphasis is on the structures which have been devised for reaching decisions. These structures constitute the essence of the guidance put forward. We have identified six key decisions. These are the decisions which occur again and again and together form the greater part of the major decisions which magistrates deal with. They have been expressed in a form which we think is simple and clear and which magistrates will find suitable in moving from one stage of the decision to another. As far as possible we have used laymen's language rather than lawyer's jargon, although we acknowledge that this is less precise and capable of a variety of interpretations. We can only hope that magistrates when using the guide will appreciate the principles on which it is based and adapt it to their needs rather than slavishly follow its guidance.

Of course, the decisions reached by magistrates will constitute the substance of justice and the courts have a responsibility for making sure that their members have the appropriate advice. The next obligation upon magistrates, after having received such advice, is to go on to consider carefully but expeditiously the essential issues on which a decision must be based. Since those issues are common for each category of decision it seems appropriate to formulate in advance these issues, to put them in the appropriate order to make them available as a guide for lay magistrates. That is what this guide seeks to do. Magistrates are free to follow its guidance or to formulate their own procedures. It is our experience that when this is done there is a greater participation by members in the decision making process and a greater concentration on those issues which are fundamental to the quality of justice.

Kerry Barker
John Sturges

May 1986

Contents

		Page
Chapter 1:	The decision making process	1
Chapter 2:	The verdict decision	6
Chapter 3:	The sentencing decision	11
Chapter 4:	A submission of "no case to answer"	23
Chapter 5:	The adjournment decision	26
Chapter 6:	The bail decision	30
Chapter 7:	Mode of trial decisions	37
Chapter 8:	The role of the chairman	40
Chapter 9:	The court clerk	45
Appendix	Sample cases	53

Chapter 1

The decision making process

There are several ways of looking at the work which magistrates do, and one which has come to be widely accepted emphasises decision making. The hearing of cases can be viewed as a series of decisions which follow a pre-determined sequence. Many of the decisions which magistrates are required to make are of an essentially routine character and usually such decisions do not present much difficulty. But others are not routine. They call for very careful consideration and allow for the exercise of considerable discretion. These are often of great consequence to the persons concerned in the case and are important in establishing the quality of justice as seen by the public. Although justice is an abstract concept it is made concrete in the decisions which are reached in specific cases of which offenders and the public are made aware.

1. Collective decisions

In most magistrates' courts these decisions are not individual; a court usually consists of three lay magistrates and the decisions are collective in character. Of course, magistrates play their part in this process in an individual capacity by making up their minds, but they move on from this preliminary stage in decision making to an interchange of views until the decision reached is a collective one.

It is true that one of their number acts as a chairman and serves as their spokesman, but each magistrate has an equal responsibility for the decisions which are reached

1

and feels an obligation to consider the views of his colleagues and attempt to reconcile differences. Of course, such differences can ultimately be resolved by a majority decision and although individual members may exercise a powerful influence there is usually an open discussion in an endeavour to reach some sort of consensus. Such a process involves interaction between members and group dynamics become a factor which will influence the outcome to some extent. All of this emphasises the collective nature of decision making – a very different process from individual decision making. At every stage there is the potential for three different views and the attempt to resolve these makes for a fairly complex process.

2. Type of decision

Court decisions are reached in two very different settings. Firstly, there are those which are normally made in the courtroom, often by a nod of the head from members or by the passing of brief notes. It is not easy to establish effective communications between members of the bench and between them and their court clerk, especially when whispered conversations are likely to be overheard. It is for these reasons that decisions in the courtroom tend to be of a routine and subordinate nature where communication is reduced to a minimum.

When more than a minimum is necessary the bench normally retires – so it is in the retiring room that decisions requiring a fuller discussion are reached. This is a much more convenient setting for decision making and it is here that the more difficult and important decisions are considered. There is some debate as to "when to retire". Discussions with experienced magistrates have revealed that there are generally six categories of decision which are more likely to be discussed in the retiring room than in the courtroom. They are:

1. the verdict decision
2. the sentence decision

3. the adjournment decision (when contested or when delay is involved).
4. the bail decision
5. the mode of trial decision
6. the "no case to answer" decision

Of course, there are occasions when a decision within one of these categories is fairly routine, eg application for adjournment, but whenever the decision requires the consideration of several factors then the retiring room is the more appropriate place. It is the *complexity* of the decision which determines the setting in which it needs to be considered.

Again, this indicates something about the nature of decision making. Most of the "retiring room decisions" are complex because there are a number of important issues which must be carefully considered and the identification of these issues is itself an important stage in decision making. Only then can each be considered fully.

But identification of issues and their careful consideration is not the only factor in complex decision making. Just as important is the order in which each issue is considered. There is an appropriate order which is dictated by the nature of the decision. In considering a verdict decision it is often clear that issues of law have to be settled before considerations of evidence and so it is with most decisions. The order in which identified issues are considered is crucial to the decision making process.

It is also true that retiring room decisions are complex not only because there are several issues which must be considered in a proper order but because there are three members who must consider each issue. They are likely to have differing views. A measure of agreement is necessary before moving on to the next stage. This is best illustrated in the case of verdict decisions which arise from long disputed cases. A certain period for reflection is necessary in a case which may have lasted for several hours. There is the need to check through members' notes of the case, sometimes requiring the assistance of the clerk's notes. There is the need to sift through the evidence to separate the evidence which is agreed from that which is disputed and only then can the disputed evidence be evaluated by each of the members.

The same applies to a sentencing decision and this is often complicated by having to consider several offences, and in some cases several offenders. The complexity of such decisions requires a retiring room setting for proper consideration to take place.

3. Method

Very often the method used to consider complex decisions is open discussion. It has come to be regarded as the obvious method, natural and democratic since it allows each member to make such contribution to the discussion as he or she feels able. But it can be a very frustrating experience. Discussion is supposed to identify and clarify issues but the reiteration of views can lead to greater confusion. Open discussion often gives scope for a member who feels strongly on an issue to exaggerate its importance. The same issues are discussed again and again without being resolved and without regard to their proper sequence. Again, although in theory the open discussion gives scope for every member to participate, in practice discussions are often dominated by the strongest personality. The articulate member has an advantage over the diffident member. Voting, rather than a constructive discussion which takes account of each member's views and tries to resolve differences, becomes a way of deciding. In practice open discussion is not always a satisfactory method of reaching a collective decision on complex issues.

The alternative method which has come to be adopted in some courts is "structured discussion". It is the method which tries to establish order and relevance to each part of the discussion: to concentrate on those things which are important, to attempt some sort of resolution of differences as the bench moves from one stage of the decision to another, and to take account of each member's views at all stages of the process. On balance it also enables decisions to be reached more quickly. "Structured discussion" has distinct advantages and it is not surprising that a number of experienced magistrates have tried to adopt this method, replacing the open discussion by a more structured approach.

But there are difficulties when individual magistrates try and do this. The more insistent an individual is that he has discovered the right approach the more likely is resistance from other members. Surely what is necessary is for a general agreement that a structured approach is useful and then for magistrates to begin to work out appropriate structures for each category of decision. This is a process in which the whole bench needs to be involved. An attempt to work out what are the key issues in each category of decision, to point out the questions which must be resolved and to determine the order in which they must be considered ought not to be beyond the capacity of any group of experienced lay magistrates. After all lay magistrates in courts all over the country are reaching these decisions every day. There is an enormous body of experience to draw on. In this respect magistrates are experts for they have been doing it for years. In recent times training exercises in several parts of the country have taken place in an effort to encourage magistrates to do this.

In the following Chapters structures have been devised and are boldly put forward as suggestions which might prove helpful. In them have been incorporated some of the suggestions made by experienced lay magistrates, stipendiary magistrates and judges working in various parts of the country. Some suggestions have been rejected because they seemed too complicated. However, a wider discussion among magistrates of appropriate structures would be welcomed. The structures in this book are the result of considerable discussion – they are published in order to promote deeper consideration of issues involved. Hopefully they are simple and easily understood, an essential quality for any practice which is to be widely accepted by lay magistrates. Once used the method of structured discussion could be openly examined and many more appropriate structures might be formulated.

Chapter 2

The verdict decision

Magistrates are very much aware of the consequences that flow from a verdict decision, and approach every not guilty plea case with great care. It is often assumed that for this reason such cases are very difficult. However, many magistrates after some experience on the bench find them less difficult than many sentence or bail decisions. This is in part because guilty or not guilty seems a simple decision which ought to be resolved fairly easily by any magistrate. The all important question "wonderfully concentrates the mind" and focuses attention throughout the hearing. This question is uppermost and at the conclusion of the case there is a readiness to come to a decision. Indeed the phrase "there is not much doubt in this case" is more frequently used about verdict decisions than any other.

Yet upon analysis decisions are seldom simple. In contested cases there may be a long hearing with several witnesses being called by both sides, each subject to the difficult process of cross examination and sometimes re-examination. Many many words will have been spoken, some of them by persons who do not express themselves very clearly and often by witnesses who do not appreciate the importance of what they are saying. Much of the evidence may be of a conflicting character, so it is somewhat surprising that lay magistrates sometimes without further consideration express themselves as having "no doubt". Examples of the dangers involved can be given.

The readiness to reach a decision soon after the completion of the hearing will almost certainly cause the retiring room discussion to appear perfunctory. It is only in those cases where there is considerable uncertainty or downright disagreement that a fuller discussion takes place with a more detailed consideration of the important issues. Even then it is often in the form of one member affirming his decision with other members seeking to challenge the reasons for it. It is likely that there will be a mixture of disagreement, some members in conflict on the law, or about the evidence, or about the trustworthiness of witnesses, or about what has to be proved. These, and other, subordinate issues will be considered in open discussion, although the need to consider them one at a time and in a proper sequence may be disregarded because the focal point will be on the member who has already made up his mind.

It is the assumption that lay magistrates, after hearing a case, ought to have little difficulty in making up their minds that leads them to reach the ultimate stage before they have considered the subordinate stages in the verdict decision. All of these deserve proper attention before the substantive decision can be reached and the expectation that members will be able to give a decision immediately upon their retirement is not soundly based because it ignores the complexity of such decisions. To decide "guilty" or "not guilty" is the very last stage in the process and the undue emphasis on the decision reached immediately the hearing is completed needs to give way to a more ordered and deliberative approach. It is for this reason that a suitable structure is suggested.

1. The standard of proof

It is always worthwhile to begin every discussion of a verdict decision with a reminder of the standard of proof which is required. Although the words "beyond reasonable doubt" are frequently used it is not so certain that the high standard implied by these words is sufficiently appreciated. It is considerably higher than we expect in most areas of human activity. Moreover, the prosecution is normally required to prove every part of the charge according to this high standard. In those infrequent cases when the burden of proof falls upon the defence (and in civil cases) the balance of probabilities is sufficient − a much lower standard. It is essential to establish this from the beginning.

2. The law

Every case derives from a charge and every charge derives from a particular provision of the law. Each offence contains certain essential elements and to establish these at an early stage is important. Usually the prosecution will have outlined these at the commencement of the hearing and if there is any doubt the bench can always ask to be reminded of them. What has to be proved, and the elements which are being disputed, need to be agreed by all members and the advice of the court clerk sought at this stage if necessary.

3. The evidence

The next stage is to consider the evidence. In magistrates' courts there is an almost total reliance on oral evidence so that the notes made by each member together with those of their court clerk will serve to refresh memories. It is then that the identification of the various pieces of evidence can take place and a separation of what is agreed and what is disputed is the next stage. All the members need to be satisfied that they recognise separate parts of the evidence. Very often this analytical approach reveals very little in dispute and therefore consideration can be concentrated upon that part of the case where there is a conflict.

4. Evaluation of evidence

Having established what needs to be proved, and having identified the evidence, an evaluation can take place. This will resolve itself into a fairly simple question as to whom to believe and how far was the evidence substantiated or supported by other evidence. It is at this stage that there is scope for considerable disagreement and a discussion as to why certain pieces of evidence were accepted while others were rejected is a valuable exercise in assessment. It is then that agreement is possible on the worth of the evidence which is accepted.

5. Verdict

When the evidence is evaluated and agreement reached the bench is in a position to proceed to verdict. The facts have been established from the assessment of evidence and these can be matched against the various elements that constitute the charge; from this a decision can be reached. There may still be grounds for some differences particularly when the high standard of proof required is considered, and in the end it may be a majority decision. If a majority still has a doubt the charge must be dismissed. If the majority find the case proved "beyond reasonable doubt" the decision is guilty. But the decision will have been reached not on the basis of an "overall impression" but after a full consideration of all the matters that are appropriate.

6. Reasons

It is at this stage that members may wish to go beyond what is required of them. The pronouncement in court will not normally include any other comment, but members may find it helpful to formulate the reasons for the decision. A summary of the findings is always helpful and will serve to confirm that all the relevant issues have been properly considered and these can then be recorded so that they are available should the decision go to appeal.

It is in the retiring room that verdict decisions are normally reached and this is an ideal setting for using a structured approach. It enables members to be satisfied that the charge as brought has been proved beyond reasonable doubt and that they have been able to play their part at all stages through to the substantive decision itself.

THE VERDICT – GUILTY OR NOT GUILTY
A STRUCTURED APPROACH

STANDARD OF PROOF
What is the standard of proof required in this case –
Beyond reasonable doubt?
or a balance of probabilities?

THE LAW
What are the legal elements of the offence?
How many of those were in dispute?
Do we need the clerk's assistance to identify them?

EVIDENCE
Have we got good notes or will we need the assistance
of the clerk's notes?
What was agreed?
What was in dispute?

EVALUATION
How do we evaluate the disputed evidence?
Whom do we believe?
Is there any independent support?

VERDICT
Can we now agree on a verdict?
Will it have to be a majority decision?

REASONS
What are the reasons for our verdict?
Could we set this out briefly if we had to do so for an
appeal?

Chapter 3

The sentencing decision

Making decisions on sentence is the most important part of a magistrate's decision making experience. Such decisions directly affect offenders and have considerable influence on the impression which the public has of the effectiveness of the work done in the courts. It is also a fact that sentencing decisions are the ones which most frequently confront magistrates; apart from the great volume of cases heard in magistrates' courts, most defendants – over 80% – plead guilty. Indeed magistrates are "sentencers" and will have greater experience of sentencing than of any other type of decision.

Such decisions cover a very wide range of offenders. The type and nature of the decision can vary enormously from the routine imposition of a fine for a common offence with which magistrates are very familiar and of which they have much experience – the speeding motorist comes to mind – to the extremely complicated, involving difficult and technical offences with a myriad of factors both mitigating and aggravating.

In dealing with this range, lay magistrates are confronted with a large number of alternative sentences with very different criteria applying to each. The sentencing decision can often require the magistrates to make a number of choices and since those choices must be made by three magistrates endeavouring to reach some sort of agreement, many sentencing decisions can be regarded as complex.

An agreed agenda for consideration should be a very helpful aid to sentencing and at the end of the Chapter is put forward a structure for the sentencing decision which could be adopted by lay magistrates dealing with the more difficult or non-routine case.

The structure is drawn from both experience and the guidelines issued or practices adopted by the appellate courts. That point is important because the method to be used to reach the sentencing decision has been well considered and must not be ignored by lay magistrates – it forms part of the law on sentencing. Not only is it important to ensure that all the vital ingredients of the sentencing decision have been considered but also that they have been considered in the correct sequence. That having been said the structure put forward should commend itself on the basis of its logical approach – just as the decisions of the appellate court are based upon reason.

In reaching a decision on sentence the following factors need to be considered and in the order in which they are set out:

1. The offence – how serious is it?

Here the issue is the type of offence and its seriousness. Where in the range of seriousness does this offence come in relation to all types of offence and, within its own category, how does this offence relate to other offences of the same type. To place this particular case in a range of seriousness is a crucial part of the decision making process.

In this part there are many issues to consider but most experienced magistrates will be used to thinking about them. They will often have heard a good number of cases of this particular type and will have heard a good deal about the circumstances surrounding the case in question. They will take into account any aggravating factors, such as the deliberate or "professional" nature of the offence, the age of the victim, the use of violence, breach of trust, and also such mitigating factors as provocation, peer group pressures and sudden impulse. Mitigating factors must relate only to the offence and not to the offender at this stage.

Other factors, such as the prevalence of the offence in the locality, local circumstances and the number of offences committed, should also be considered at this stage to allow a view as to the seriousness to be formed. Many benches will have considered the relative seriousness of common offences such as theft from shops, theft of cars, taking cars without consent, assaults of various types, burglary, fraud, obtaining by deception, driving with excess alcohol and driving whilst disqualified, and will have already formulated guidance or practice to promote a consistent approach to sentencing.

Having decided how serious the *type* of offence is, the next problem will be to decide how serious is this particular case given the seriousness of this category of offence. In other words where should the case be "pitched". In assault, for example, the degree of seriousness is crucial and will cause the range of seriousness to overlap many other categories; likewise, cases involving breach of trust, theft and burglary – all common offences.

To assist courts to judge the level of seriousness various tests have been suggested: "How much harm was done?" "How much gain was made?" More recently criminologists have tried to trace the connection between criminal responsibility and certain moral principles and have put forward the idea of "blameworthiness". Many lay magistrates will feel that they can assess the seriousness of an offence by using these tests.

The sentencing decision, therefore, will begin with a consideration of the particular offence with a view to assessing its seriousness in the light of the many considerations suggested. All of these can be built into a structured approach which when used as a guide may serve to remind magistrates of them and leave the magistrates to attach whatever weight to any one of them they judge appropriate.

2. Penalties – a provisional decision

Having reached some sort of consensus on how the offence is to be regarded there is the need to examine the penalties available, and to make a provisional decision as to the correct and appropriate sentence for the offence. Sentencers are given certain powers. These are the maximum penalties prescribed by law and there may be suggested penalties in the form of bench norms. There will also be guidance from the higher courts which, if not generally known, should be provided by the clerk of the court.

It is in the light of these considerations that magistrates can decide the sentence or the penalty which seems appropriate in this particular case.

It is important to make a provisional decision at this stage not only to assist with the clarity of the decision making (or thinking) process but also to prevent confusion later and the possibility that in considering the factors to follow the true seriousness of the offence will be forgotten. Such confusion can often result in a defendant being sentenced on his record and not on the offence before the court or, for example, the custodial sentence when suspended being greater than it would have been had the sentence been one of immediate imprisonment. To make a provisional decision based upon the facts of the offence is an important step which should not be missed.

3. The offender

Every offence is committed by an offender and it is the offender who is ultimately to be sentenced. So the next step is to consider the likely effect of the provisional sentence upon this particular offender. To look at the offender as an individual is crucial to the sentencing process.

What sort of person is he and what is his background. Have the magistrates been able to assess his attitude to the offence and are there any mitigating personal circumstances that should be taken into account. In assessing such factors magistrates may have observed his demeanour in court, heard from him or his solicitor or counsel, or received a report from the probation officer and others. If all of this is sufficient they are in a position to consider the offender in the light of the offence he has committed.

Of course, they will take into account his record. If he has no previous record this is to his credit. If he has a record then how relevant is it. Are the previous offences of the same type or different and how long ago were they committed. In due course, the nature of that record may confirm the court in its way of thinking of dealing with the particular offence.

Likewise, the offender's attitude to the offence is important. Was guilt confessed and when – immediately upon questioning or only when the case got to court. It is obviously right that a plea of guilty should count in favour of the offender because that is clearly in the public interest, but a last minute plea entered when all the witnesses have been gathered at court for the trial cannot be of the same value as an immediate confession and show of remorse. Equally, however, a denial of guilt should not lead to a higher sentence. It is the remorseful offender who is entitled to a "discount". This consideration is a further point in favour of making a provisional decision as to sentence before going on to consider the offender.

A structured decision needs to allow for such consideration to be given to the particular offender.

4. Objectives of sentencing

A number of possible objectives can be identified and magistrates need to consider seriously which of these should apply in a particular case. This is important because different objectives call for different types of sentence. Perhaps any guidance should identify these and remind magistrates that the recognised purposes of sentencing are to show society's abhorrence of a particular crime by way of punishment, to deter the offender or other possible offenders, to protect society or to rehabilitate the particular offender. All are possible objectives and sometimes more than one can be pursued in a particular sentence. To sentence without an objective in mind is a purposeless exercise and not worthy of a court of law.

5. Options

Having considered sentencing objectives the options which are available become a proper consideration. Some options will be ruled out because of age or physical and mental condition. Then from the remaining options a choice can be made in the light of the sentencing objective that seems appropriate, the provisional decision which was considered appropriate for the offence and the situation of the offender.

6. Further considerations

There follow upon any principal sentencing decision other considerations such as the length of sentence or the size of a fine. These matters normally follow decisions on the seriousness of the offence, the objectives of the court and the circumstances of the offender. Since custodial sentences and fines are the most common form of sentence it was felt appropriate to continue the structure by way of demonstration of the further considerations in these categories of sentence.

Custody

Perhaps the most important decision is whether or not to impose a custodial sentence. The maximum sentence in the more serious criminal cases heard in magistrates' courts, is six months imprisonment. However, magistrates have been urged seriously to consider alternatives. Moreover, even if a custodial sentence seems necessary magistrates have been asked to consider how short the term of imprisonment can be, whether it should be suspended in part or in full and for how long.

If it is decided that an alternative to custody is possible, then again a range of options presents itself, including community service, probation orders and hospital orders. In all of these the reports which have been prepared have a decisive influence since the magistrates will need to be satisfied that the proposed order will have some prospect of success in modifying the offender's behaviour.

Fines

In the case of financial penalties care needs to be taken to ensure that the means of the offender have been properly taken into account and an adjustment made against the "bench norm" wherever appropriate. The length of time it will take the offender to pay the fine is an important factor – less than a year if possible – certainly not more. If several offences are involved, having made a provisional decision as to the appropriate fine for each, the court must then look at the totality of the aggregate sentences and consider whether the result would be truly just and appropriate.

Similar considerations will apply to virtually all sentencing options before the final decision can be made.

7. Ancillary matters

Having looked at the possibilities of a custodial sentence and the alternatives, the size of financial penalties and the like, there is then a whole series of additional matters. Breach of previous orders may have to be considered. There may be offences to be taken into consideration. In the case of motor offences there are matters of endorsement of penalty points and disqualification; in all cases, compensation and costs. All these have to be borne in mind. Some have argued that technically ancillary matters such as costs should be left until after the sentencing decision has been announced. They are right, but in practice the financial considerations involved are often an important part of the decision making process.

8. The sentence

This is the stage at which all the matters which have properly been considered in a logical sequence can be brought together to determine the sentence: the seriousness of the offence, the penalties which are available, the offender, the sentencing objectives, the options open to the bench, the possibility of custody or alternatives, the amount of the fine and any additional matters. The magistrates can then proceed to fix the sentence.

9. Reasons

It is suggested that a useful exercise is to set down the reasons for the sentence. This is to clarify the thinking of the magistrates and afford assurance that all the important factors have been properly considered.

10. Explanations

Lay magistrates are not under a duty to give reasons for their sentencing decisions except where required by statute, for example when sentencing a person under 21 to a custodial sentence, but it has been suggested that explanations are important when:

(a) other offences have been taken into consideration – specific reference should be made; or

(b) the intended sentence is severe or lenient compared with the sentence which might normally have been expected on the facts of the case.

Explanations as to the effect of certain sentences are required by statute to ensure that the defendant understands the "conditions" before he leaves the courtroom.

The drawing up of reasons or explanations is a matter for all members of the bench which has made the decision and not just for the chairman.

11. The clerk

It is clearly understood that the clerk of the court must not be a party to the final decision as to sentence but at various stages of the sentencing decision he should have been able to advise on such matters as the options provided by the law, guidance relevant to choice of penalty, and the decisions of superior courts and other authorities. The court clerk will often be better informed as to the sentences imposed by the courts in the area for similar offences and will be able to assist the court to adopt a consistent approach.

Whilst the final sentencing decision is solely the responsibility of the magistrates it is a useful precaution in all but the most routine cases to inform the clerk of the court of that decision as a final check to make sure that it is in accordance with the law. The same comment must also apply to reasons or explanations to be given under statutory requirements. The use of the clerk of the court by lay magistrates in decision making is discussed in Chapter 9.

12. The pronouncement

What is said in court is obviously important for the offender but also for others and the actual wording of the pronouncement is something that is worthy of thought by all members of the bench. If there are several offences the order in which they are announced is important.

Use of the Structure

The structured approach to the sentencing decision used in this book contains many of the factors which have to be considered when deciding sentence. It is hoped that the order in which they are considered is not only logical but helpful. The object of the structure is to ensure that all relevant factors are properly considered and to assist lay magistrates in identifying them.

Other structures could be devised with changes in emphasis. Virtually every conceivable permutation could be included at great length. It is perhaps more important to adopt the principal features and sequence than rigidly to go through every point. The sequence — seriousness of offence — provisional decision — circumstances of the offender — objectives — sentence — is the key to unlocking sentencing decisions. In many cases when it is apparent from the first stage that, for example, a fine is the appropriate sentence, many of the sequential steps can be missed out. The process once adopted can be very swift and should not slow down decision making in the court.

Indeed it is firmly believed that the opposite is true — a belief supported by experience.

The structure provides an agenda for discussion in those complex cases where a whole variety of factors is deserving of consideration. Its use should be a matter for agreement by each bench just as the Magistrates' Association's "Suggestions for Traffic Offence Penalties" has come to be accepted and improved or elaborated at local bench levels.

When the Association produced its guidelines it was wise to make suggestions concerning the penalties in traffic cases. The public were most conscious of differences in penalties for these offences. Moreover, the usual penalty was a fine and thus differences were easily identified. Since then a number of benches have gone beyond this range of offences and provided for themselves suggestions for other offences, such as theft, frauds, violence etc. In most cases the suggestions have been in the form of a starting point whether expressed in terms of monetary penalty or in one or other of the options available for such offences. At least one area (involving two benches) has gone far beyond this and provided a more sophisticated guide. A Penalties Working Party has identified most of the offences which come before the two benches — some 450 — and has suggested not a "starting point" but a "range of penalty". This range applies to a married man (with two children) earning an average wage and allows deviations from the suggested range according to different circumstances. The Working Party reviews the suggestions biannually and incorporates modifications suggested by magistrates from time to time. In the area of sentencing, whilst consistency was the major concern, there is now a positive move to provide assistance to magistrates in coping with the very wide range of offences, the still growing number of alternatives which exist and on the way in which appropriate sentencing decisions can be made.

It is to be hoped that many more benches will provide for themselves sentencing guides and sentencing decision structures. The aim of all concerned must be uniformity of approach to sentencing.

THE SENTENCING DECISION –
A STRUCTURED APPROACH

THE OFFENCE
How serious is it?
Are there any aggravating factors?
(the deliberate or professional nature of the offence;
the prevalence of the offence in the locality;
breach of trust etc.)
How much harm was done?
How much gain was made?
Are there any mitigating factors
(such as provocation, outside pressures etc)?

THE PENALTIES
– A PROVISIONAL DECISION
What are our powers?
What is the maximum sentence?
What is the Bench norm?
Is there any legal guidance (from higher courts etc)?
Without considering the individual offender what
sentence would we impose for the offence?

THE OFFENDER
What is the personal background (family situation etc)?
What is his attitude to the offence?
Are there any mitigating factors?
If so, are we going to take them into account?
Do we need the help of a social enquiry report?
What will be the likely effect of our provisional
sentence on this offender?

SENTENCING OBJECTIVES
Is our primary aim to punish?
Or to rehabilitate?
Or to deter?
Or to protect society?
Or to compensate the victim?

OPTIONS
What options are open to the Bench?
Can any be ruled out because of the nature of the
offence?
Which option is most likely to secure our objective?

FURTHER CONSIDERATIONS
IF WE FIND THAT OUR SENTENCE INVOLVES CUSTODY –
How short can it be?
Is it possible to suspend it?
Is it possible to suspend part of it?
Is it not better to fix the term in days?

IF WE INTEND TO IMPOSE A FINANCIAL PENALTY
Have we carefully considered the offender's means and ability to pay?
Can the compensation, costs or fines be paid within a year?
Have we looked at the totality of the situation in the case of aggregated fines?

ANCILLARY MATTERS
Is the defendant in breach of any other sentences?
Do we have to deal with disqualification or endorsements and penalty points?
Is compensation due to anyone and can he afford to pay?
Are costs appropriate?

SENTENCE
What is to be the sentence?

REASONS
What are our reasons?

EXPLANATIONS
Are any explanations needed
(eg for a sentence which is more severe/more lenient than usual)?

CHECK WITH THE CLERK

THE PRONOUNCEMENT

Chapter 4

A submission of "no case to answer"

Once all the evidence for the prosecution (or the complainant, as the prosecutor is called in civil cases) has been heard the court may dismiss the case on its own assessment or on a submission of no case to answer, if it believes that it need not go on to hear the defence case.

Lay magistrates have been criticised for being too reluctant to take this course. Many suspect a shroud of legal mystery. Whilst clearly "the law" is always involved in deciding whether or not the defendant does have a case to answer, that decision often rests upon the magistrates' evaluation of the evidence before them and their decision as to its credibility – issues with which they are very used to dealing when reaching verdict decisions.

Once the "no case to answer" decision is broken down into its constituent parts, and provided that all legal questions have been properly set down and clarified, the mystery will disappear. A structured approach to the decision as to whether or not there is a case to answer will leave most lay magistrates feeling quite at ease with the decision making process.

The structure put forward is based upon legal practice and judicial experience and also the guidance set down by the High Court. In 1962 a Practice Note directed that in criminal cases:

> "Without attempting to lay down any principle of law, we think that as a matter of practice justices should be guided by the following considerations. A submission that there is no case to answer may

properly be made and upheld (a) when there has been no evidence to prove an essential element in the alleged offence; (b) when the evidence adduced by the prosecution has been so discredited as the result of cross-examination or is so manifestly unreliable that no reasonable tribunal could safely convict on it. Apart from these two situations a tribunal should not in general be called upon to reach a decision as to conviction or acquittal until the whole of the evidence which either side wishes to tender has been placed before it. If however a submission is made that there is no case to answer, the decision should depend not so much on whether the adjudicating tribunal (if compelled to do so) would at that stage convict or acquit but on whether the evidence is such that a reasonable tribunal might convict. If a reasonable tribunal might convict on the evidence so far laid before it, there is a case to answer." ([1962] 1 All ER 448).

Each step in the structure suggested is an independent step and the sequence is important. Progress through the structure depends upon the answer to each step so that, for example, if it is found that an element of an offence is not supported by any evidence then a decision that there is not a case to answer must be made without further ado. The role of the chairman in ensuring that only relevant matters are taken into account and that time is not wasted, again becomes important – most of these decisions having to be made in the retiring room.

"NO CASE TO ANSWER" DECISIONS
A STRUCTURED APPROACH

[Once all the evidence for the prosecution has been heard the court may dismiss the case *either of its own motion* or on a submission of no case to answer.]

WHAT ARE THE ELEMENTS OF THE OFFENCE?
Have we had them set out for us in court —
by the prosecution, the defence or the clerk?
Can we list each of the necessary ingredients, ie elements, or do we need the clerk's assistance
to do that?

WHAT ABOUT THE EVIDENCE?
Have we received supporting evidence for each element?
If the answer is "no" then there is not a case to answer.

If there is evidence to support each element of the offence
(1) Was any of that evidence discredited in cross examination?
or (2) Was any of that evidence clearly unreliable?

No matter what final decision we might make in this case —

COULD A REASONABLE BENCH CONVICT ON THE REMAINING EVIDENCE
(ie THAT WHICH WAS NOT SO DISCREDITED OR NOT FOUND TO BE CLEARLY UNRELIABLE)?
If the answer is "yes" and there is evidence to support each element then there is a case to answer.

ARE WE CERTAIN THAT WE HAVE GOT THE LAW RIGHT?
Check with the clerk

CAN WE AGREE ON THE PRONOUNCEMENT
"We find that there is a case to answer"
or
"we do not find that there is a case to answer and so the case will be dismissed."

[In committal proceedings the case would not be "dismissed" at this stage, nor would a committal to the Crown Court automatically follow — for the special procedures involved in committals check with the clerk.]

Chapter 5

The adjournment decision

An all too frequent decision in magistrates' courts, the decision to adjourn the hearing of a case, can be said to have disproportionately little attention paid to it. The majority of adjournment decisions are made at the request or with the consent of the parties to the case, and most often without enquiry by the court.

It is also true to say that when discussing matters without reference to individual cases all parties would agree that delay is inimical to justice and should be avoided whenever possible. The facts of life dictate, however, that in most cases the only disinterested party is the court itself and that if the court (magistrates and their advisers) does not take steps to reduce or prevent delays then little is likely to be achieved.

The problem for most magistrates is the wish to be fair and to act in the interests of justice. Perceptions of what is fair or in the interests of justice can vary widely and these matters surely deserve a disciplined rather than a free approach. The acceptance by a bench of a structured approach to making adjournment decisions would not only introduce discipline, but also lead to general fairness by ensuring consistency. Such a move would also create a general awareness by practitioners of the standards of the court and lead to improvements in the preparation and presentation of both the cases themselves and applications for adjournments.

Most applications for adjournments are simple and unarguable. The result will be almost inevitable and will demand little by way of enquiry by the court — for example adjournments for social enquiry reports; for driving licences to be sent to the court; for notices to be properly served; or for witnesses to be called when a not guilty plea has been entered without prior warning or when it was known that at the first hearing witnesses would not be available.

In most cases, however, the court should satisfy itself that an adjournment is both appropriate and fair. Adjournment decisions should not be automatic. The use of a structured approach would ensure proper consideration and raise the kind of questions which need to be asked whenever applications for adjournments fall to be considered.

Natural justice demands that each party has an opportunity to present his or her case. It does not demand repeated opportunities nor does it require the court to "bend over backwards" towards one party or another in order to be seen to be fair. A Home Office Working Party when looking at the problem of delays in magistrates' courts had this to say:

> "Magistrates are sometimes said to be too ready to grant adjournments stemming from a laudable but often misdirected concern for the rights of the defendant. Delay is usually not to the defendant's advantage. Some courts have found it possible where a date of hearing has been fixed to go ahead with a case where the defence request for a further adjournment is not accepted as reasonable or to dismiss a case where the prosecution's request is similarly unacceptable".

Some courts have adopted a test of reasonableness when deciding upon adjournments: others use foreseeability as their yardstick. A full investigation would involve both these concepts. It is hoped that the structure embodies all that is required for a court to be fair and act in accordance with the principles of natural justice.

ADJOURNMENT DECISIONS
A STRUCTURED APPROACH

[A decision to adjourn a case is often looked upon as automatic – it should never be
– if delays are to be controlled the court must take care over every application for an adjournment]

WHAT IS THE HISTORY OF THIS CASE?
How many times has it been listed before?
What was the expectation of the court for today's hearing?
How much time have the parties had to prepare for today's hearing?
Is the defendant in custody or on bail?

WHAT ARE THE REASONS FOR THE APPLICATION?
Are those reasons relevant?
Were those matters foreseeable and,
if so,
what steps have been taken to avoid the need for a further adjournment?
Has the court been contacted and was the other side told before today?

IS ANY FURTHER DELAY REASONABLE?
What has any previous court said about this?

WOULD IT BE FAIR TO BOTH SIDES TO GRANT A FURTHER ADJOURNMENT?
Are there any witnesses present?
Who was to blame for the case not being ready?
Would an adjournment be clearly unfair to anybody?

IF AN ADJOURNMENT IS REFUSED – WHAT MIGHT HAPPEN?
Can the case proceed without a missing witness?
Would 30 minutes or so allow the solicitor to take instructions?
Would a short delay enable a witness to be brought to court?
If the prosecution cannot put evidence before us will the consequence be a *dismissal*

or
are we sitting as examining justices when the
consequence will be a *discharge*?

IF AN ADJOURNMENT IS TO BE GRANTED – WHAT NEED WE
SAY?
How long is reasonable? (Any adjournment should be
for the shortest possible time.)
Should we insist that the case proceed next time?
Should we express our displeasure in public or
privately?
Can the court accommodate the case on the proposed
date?

CAN WE AGREE ON THE PRONOUNCEMENT?
Do we need to check anything else with the clerk?

[The Home Office Working Party when looking at the
problem of delays in magistrates' courts had this to say:

"Magistrates are sometimes said to be too ready to grant
adjournments stemming from a laudable but often mis-
directed concern for the rights of the defendant.

Delay is usually not to the defendant's advantage.

Some courts have found it possible where a date of
hearing has been fixed to go ahead with a case where the
defence request for a further adjournment is not accepted
as reasonable or to dismiss a case where the prosecution's
request is similarly unacceptable."]

Chapter 6

The bail decision

Of all the decisions taken by magistrates the bail decision is the most tightly circumscribed by statute. It was to this decision that Parliament paid particular attention when enacting the Bail Act 1976 so that the steps to be followed when making a bail decision are virtually laid down in the Act. Also the law requires magistrates to formulate and announce their reasons for withholding bail or granting bail subject to conditions (conditional bail) – a process with which most lay magistrates are by now very familiar.

Having said all that, the bail decision is particularly important because it affects the liberty of an individual before the guilt of that person has been determined. A decision to keep in custody a person who is innocent can have the most drastic affect on that person's life – going far beyond the consequences of most sentencing decisions made in magistrates' courts. So it was perhaps right that Parliament should have laid down precise steps to be followed.

One of the major problems facing magistrates, however, is that bail decisions usually have to be made on the basis of submissions and arguments – not on evidence. When the question of whether or not to withhold bail is being considered the answer is rarely based upon findings of fact as in verdict or sentence decisions, but rather on suggestions and speculation often based upon history rather than current activity. That problem was recognised by Parliament when it imposed the crucial test "are there substantial grounds for believing . . .".

"Substantial grounds for believing" is a difficult concept

to define and is certainly not the same as the standards of proof which lay magistrates are used to dealing with — "beyond reasonable doubt" and "balance of probabilities". Since those two standards are based upon findings of facts after hearing evidence, the standard of "substantial grounds for believing", having heard only argument and proposition, can be said to be a somewhat lower standard.

The "substantial grounds for believing" test only applies to those cases in which the court is considering withholding bail. If a remand in custody is out of the question, because of the type of offence for example, then conditions can be attached to bail but the test then is simply "are they necessary" for one of the statutory reasons. It is important to realise that there are two different tests for bail decisions and two different sets of circumstances in which they are to be used. Very often courts get confused about this — often having been misled by the advocates who have not addressed themselves to this difference. Even more important is the need to remember that it is the court which has the responsibility for the decision and that the decision can and often should be made upon grounds considered by the court which were not put forward by the prosecution. There are many reasons why it will not be in the interests of the police to oppose bail. It is quite proper for the police and those representing them to take those reasons into account but just as proper for the court to consider them not relevant to the decision the court has to make. If, however, the court has considered grounds or matters which have not been canvassed in court then the accused and his advocate must be given the opportunity of addressing the court on those grounds or matters before a final decision is made.

Turning to the structure imposed by Parliament, magistrates will find that there are three distinct parts of the process. First, decisions have to be made on the preliminary matters: has a full bail decision already been made — that is a bail decision having heard full arguments on the question; if so, have the circumstances changed since that decision was made — is the accused in custody for another reason perhaps. Second, the major question of whether or not to grant bail, based on different considerations, depending upon whether the alleged offence is imprisonable or not. The third part comes into play sometimes as an alternative to the possibility of withholding bail, and is the question of whether or not conditions are necessary.

The distinction between the second and third parts is important; it is too often blurred in the courtroom especially when the accused or his representative are suggesting that bail conditions are appropriate and will be complied with. Practical problems do arise when courts consider conditions before the primary test in any case when that test has to be applied. If there are not substantial grounds for believing that the accused will fail to answer bail, will commit further offences or will interfere with the course of justice, then logically conditions will not be necessary. Only when the court has found that substantial grounds for believing that one or more grounds for refusing bail do exist should it then consider whether the fears involved can be met by conditions rather than custody.

It will be in comparatively rare circumstances that the question of withholding bail does not arise but the court will need to go on to the third part of the process to consider whether bail conditions are necessary.

As with all decisions, a structure is important but in the case of the bail decision it is vital that the correct sequence is followed to avoid illogical and unnecessary decisions. The only remaining problem for lay magistrates is to decide whether all relevant matters have been considered. It is suggested that the question and answer approach is a very helpful way of overcoming the problem and the structure proposed is set out that way.

The bail decision structure is lengthy; the legal situation requires that all the stages be considered. It should, however, be simple to use with the majority of questions requiring only yes or no answers. Most lay magistrates will be quite used to the process, after having applied most or parts of the structure themselves and it is hoped that they will feel confident to use the structure both as an aid when sorting the wheat from the chaff of advocates' submissions, and as a check list for use in the retiring room.

The starting point must always be the accused's right to bail.

BAIL OR CUSTODY
A STRUCTURED DECISION

Remember – The Bail Act gives the defendant a right to unconditional bail (in all but the rarest cases)

WHAT IS THE ALLEGED OFFENCE?

IS THE DEFENDANT ON BAIL OR IN CUSTODY AT THE MOMENT?
Whose decision was that?

HAS ANOTHER COURT ALREADY FOUND THAT GROUNDS FOR REFUSING BAIL EXIST?
What were those grounds?
Does the *Nottingham Justices'* case apply?
Has anyone suggested that the situation has changed?

IF SO, HAS THE SITUATION CHANGED SINCE THE LAST BAIL DECISION WAS MADE?
Are the changes relevant?
Do we have to make a decision as to bail or custody?

DOES THE DEFENDANT NEED TO BE KEPT IN CUSTODY FOR HIS OWN PROTECTION (WELFARE IF A JUVENILE)?
What are our reasons?

IS THE DEFENDANT ALREADY IN CUSTODY SERVING A SENTENCE?

HAVE WE GOT SUFFICIENT INFORMATION ABOUT THE CASE AND THE DEFENDANT
– IF NOT WAS IT PRACTICABLE TO OBTAIN SUCH INFORMATION BEFORE THE COURT HEARING?
What are our reasons?

HAS THE DEFENDANT BEEN ARRESTED FOR ABSCONDING OR BREAKING THE CONDITIONS OF HIS BAIL IMPOSED AT AN EARLIER HEARING?

Is the offence imprisonable? if so:

ARE THERE *SUBSTANTIAL* GROUNDS FOR BELIEVING THAT:

1. The defendant will fail to surrender to custody?
What are our reasons?
How serious is the offence?
How strong is the evidence?

What kind of sentence is likely?
Has the defendant been on bail before? Did he answer it?
What kind of lifestyle does he lead? Has he got a fixed address?
Are there any other reasons?
Would bail with conditions be effective — instead of custody?

2. *The defendant will commit an offence whilst on bail?*
What are our reasons?
What is involved in this offence?
Are there previous convictions which suggest that further offences might be committed?
Has he committed an offence whilst on bail this time or before?
Are there any other reasons?
Would bail with conditions be effective — instead of custody?

3. *The defendant will interfere with witnesses or in some other way obstruct the course of justice?*
What are our reasons?
What is the nature of the case?
What kind of evidence is involved?
Is there any strong evidence that he will interfere with witnesses etc?
Is there a record of the defendant or his associates being involved in this kind of thing before?
Would bail with conditions be effective — instead of custody?

OR ARE WE ASKING FOR SOCIAL ENQUIRY REPORTS ETC, AND IT WOULD BE IMPRACTICABLE TO OBTAIN THEM WITHOUT KEEPING THE DEFENDANT IN CUSTODY?
What are our reasons?
Would bail with conditions be effective — instead of custody?

If the offence is not imprisonable:

HAS THE DEFENDANT PREVIOUSLY ABSCONDED AND DO WE THINK HE WILL ABSCOND AGAIN?
What are our reasons?

CAN WE REACH A DECISION?

HAVE WE FOUND THAT THERE ARE GROUNDS FOR REFUSING BAIL?
Can we set out those grounds and the reasons for our findings?

WILL CONDITIONAL BAIL SUFFICE INSTEAD OF CUSTODY?
If so — what conditions should we impose?
Is each condition relevant to a ground that we have found?
If we have found that the defendant is unlikely to answer his bail would a SURETY enable us to grant conditional bail?

IF NO GROUND FOR REFUSING BAIL HAS BEEN FOUND THEN THE DEFENDANT SHOULD BE GRANTED UNCONDITIONAL BAIL

BUT   — *If we have not considered refusing bail do we think that conditions are necessary*

- to ensure the defendant surrenders to custody?
- to prevent the defendant committing an offence whilst on bail?
- to prevent the defendant interfering with witnesses or obstructing the course of justice?

If so, what condition(s) should we impose? Are they relevant?

Note: There may also be decisions as to
- the issue of a "full bail argument" certificate;
- future remands in absence with consent;
- the acceptability of a surety

to be taken after the bail or custody decision has been made. Your clerk can advise you.

Chapter 7

Mode of trial decisions

Magistrates' courts deal with three types of offence: indictable offences which if committed by an adult can be dealt with at a Crown Court only; summary offences which can be dealt with by a magistrates' court only, and either-way offences which, if committed by an adult, can be heard either at the Crown Court or in a magistrates' court. In either-way cases the decision as to where the case should be heard lies with the magistrates and is known as a decision as to mode of trial.

The procedure involves hearing representations from the parties or their representatives as to the appropriate venue for the ultimate hearing of the case, and then a consideration of the issues and implications involved with regard to the nature of the case, its hearing and the powers of the alternative courts. The problem for most courts is the adequacy of the information upon which decisions have to be made. The straightforward "this case is suitable for summary trial" statement is clearly inadequate and the court has every right to ask for more information.

So the court needs to be informed in some detail about the nature of the case and the circumstances of the alleged offence or offences. The court must be fully aware of its powers and must pay special attention to any other factors which might make the case one more suitable for trial at the Crown Court.

In some circumstances the court can later change its mind, for example, where a not guilty plea has been entered, and before the close of the prosecution case the court decides that the case should really have gone to the

Crown Court. Such a change of mind cannot take place after a plea of guilty has been entered. Also during committal proceedings a late decision can be made to revert to summary trial.

The court's decision will not affect the accused's right to demand trial by jury in either-way cases and magistrates will be faced with a rather different type of decision whenever the accused later asks to change his mind.

The consequence for both prosecution and defence of the magistrates' decision as to mode of trial can be significant both in terms of result (verdict and sentence) and of preparation for proceedings. Those consequences justify careful consideration of the mode of trial decision but they do not justify consideration in themselves. The fact that a Crown Court trial is much more expensive or will cause many more hours of work for the investigating police officer or the Crown Prosecutor is not relevant. Similarly, consideration of the practical problems facing the defence should also be ruled out.

In certain circumstances the mode of trial decision can be made in the absence of the accused. Cases involving criminal damage can be rather complicated and the situation with regard to offences to be taken into consideration – are they part of a series of offences? or do they relate only to the offender as opposed to the offence? – has been the subject of much legal debate. The court clerk will be available to advise on these matters but in most cases the mode of trial decision should be capable of simple analysis.

Again the discipline of using a structured approach will help rule out irrelevancies and ensure that all proper matters have been considered. The emphasis is always on the offence not the offender, and whilst the wishes or representations of the parties must be considered the decision must be that of the court.

MODE OF TRIAL DECISIONS
A STRUCTURED APPROACH

[An indictable offence can be tried at the Crown Court only. A summary offence can be tried in a Magistrates' Court only. An either-way offence can be tried at either the Crown Court or the Magistrates' Court.]

WHAT IS THE OFFENCE – WHAT CATEGORY DOES IT FALL INTO?

If an either-way offence
WHAT REPRESENTATIONS HAVE THE PROSECUTOR AND THE DEFENDANT
(OR HIS ADVOCATE) MADE?
The representations should relate to the offence and circumstances relevant to it – *not to the offender*

IS THE CASE SUITABLE FOR SUMMARY TRIAL?
What is the nature of the case?
Do the circumstances make the offence a serious one?
Will our powers to deal with the offender for the offence be adequate?
Are there any other circumstances which make the case more suitable for trial at the Crown Court?

If the case is suitable for summary trial

DOES THE DEFENDANT AGREE?

If we decide that the case is not suitable for summary trial
WHAT ARE OUR REASONS?

CAN WE AGREE ON OUR PRONOUNCEMENT?

[Facts about the offender are not important at this stage. Everything is concentrated on the offence or series of offences. If it turns out that the record of the offender, or the number of cases to be taken into consideration, cause a change of mind, the offender can always be committed to the Crown Court for sentence.]

Chapter 8

The role of the chairman

Most lay magistrates aspire to be chairmen. The act of presiding in court may be thought to enhance the standing of the magistrate and to give him or her added prestige, but in reality most magistrates welcome the experience and the opportunity to do the job well. However, it is a difficult role and to be a good chairman requires special qualities. A great deal of training offered to lay magistrates has concentrated on chairmanship with the objective of cultivating those qualities. It is certainly true that when the role is performed well the work of the court runs smoothly and when it is done badly it can be disastrous. Much depends on the understanding which exists between the chairman and the court clerk and it is worth working at this relationship for it is the key to much else.

The most important attribute for chairmen is that they should feel comfortable in what they are doing and have the confidence of their colleagues. The chairman does not enjoy any additional powers, but the other magistrates require him or her to speak for them and to control the business of the court so that there is a considerate hearing of each case and so that the essential decisions are properly reached.

To feel comfortable and confident requires that the chairman should have a knowledge of the procedure of the court and be able to anticipate each stage in the hearing. This is not difficult since there is a routine pattern and a good chairman can be prepared for the next stage. When knowledge of procedure is allied to experience most chairmen can anticipate what is likely to happen: Beyond this chairmen need a good deal of information. If there is a sentencing handbook they need to be familiar with its contents. They need to be aware of the availability of certain sentencing options. They need to know something about legal aid and the working of the Duty Solicitor Scheme. A good chairman is one who has taken the trouble to acquire information about the working of the court system beyond that of other colleagues. It is from this sound basis of knowledge that the chairman is able to control the conduct of the court and secure the confidence of colleagues. Much of the necessary control derives from a knowledge of what is to happen, but an awareness that in many situations such knowledge is limited is vital. Part of the skill of maintaining control is the ability to ask questions at the right time, either of the court clerk, other magistrates or the other court practitioners. A chairman does not need to say much, but a well-timed intervention can keep the business flowing.

Chairmanship therefore has something of the flavour of a public performance and although the scope is limited it is important that is is seen to be well done. However, by far the most important duty is to see that decisions are reached. Presiding in court is a matter of ensuring that a wide range of decisions are dealt with. Some of these are of a routine character but it is important that these and other substantive matters are dealt with promptly. Also important is that such decisions are the collective decisions of the bench and seen to be so. This is not easy in the court room situation since it does not lend itself to discussion. It is for this reason that one of the more important qualities of a chairman is the ability to assess when the bench should retire. As soon as complexity, possible disagreement or the need for further elucidation is detected, the chairman should be ready to respond to a colleague's suggestion to retire, or to make such a suggestion.

It is sometimes assumed that the decision to retire eases the difficulties of the chairman's role. It is true that chairmanship in the retiring room is not subject to public scrutiny, but if anything the role becomes considerably more demanding and more important there. Magistrates' training so far has not examined closely the role of the chairman in the retiring room, but, for example, ensuring full participation of all the members is an exacting responsibility.

Traditionally, people who presided at court were often strong personalities and experience was acknowledged as giving them the right to "give a lead" in the retiring room. This often meant stating what the decision should be and securing agreement. In recent years this has been considerably modified and it is acknowledged that the strong chairman may need to be restrained. In practice this has meant that the chairman is expected to invite the most junior member for an opinion first, then the other colleague and only then attempt to summarise their views and state his or her own. This can often be just as unsatisfactory and is no guarantee that the proper issues have been fully considered.

Much of the difficulty can be overcome by the adoption of well-thought out structures of discussion. These can serve as the agreed agenda for the retiring room discussion, curtailing irrelevant considerations and concentrating on the important issues in a logical sequence. Perhaps, as has been suggested, the whole bench needs to discuss the formulation of such structures so that when they are adopted all members feel committed to them when they retire. It is hoped that the structures put forward in this book will be accepted by many benches. The retiring room discussion then concentrates on the structures without any additional need to bring order to the discussion. It is in this situation that chairmanship in the retiring room becomes a manageable operation within the competence of most lay magistrates.

The use of a structured approach to decision making should assist the chairman in several ways because chairmanship has four distinct functions. Firstly, the chairman can serve as a custodian of the structure − being there to make sure that people keep to the agenda of decision making. In doing so a chairman does not have to shape the discussion, or dominate it − simply make possible an ordered discussion. That is traditionally the role of a good chairman in any decision making body. The chairman keeps people to the agenda: concentrates attention on the relevant matters: and keeps people to the point. Now this requires considerable skill but it is a role that is readily acknowledged as being appropriate to any chairman.

The second function is that of securing maximum participation. This means enabling two colleagues to take part in the discussion at every stage in the process of decision making. To get views stated clearly and the reasons for them and the challenge of contrary views is an essential preliminary to securing consensus. It is important that each member shall feel that he has played his part.

The third function is to make sure that the bench has all the information and advice that it needs to reach a decision. This will often call for summaries of what has been said in court, and perhaps the correction of misunderstandings; in all of this the help of the court clerk will be invaluable. At what stage this help is called for will depend upon the chairman's alertness. The chairman can make sure that the same arguments are not repeated on the basis of false premises by asking the court clerk to assist on matters of law, sentencing, mixture of law and fact or any other matter which is appropriate. In this, of course, the chairman has a special responsibility to ensure that the decision is reached by the bench but that it is a decision arrived at after the best advice on appropriate matters has been taken into consideration. It is an important part of the chairman's function to make it possible for the court clerk to fulfil his or her essential function of advising the bench and then to enable the bench to go on and make its decision.

Finally, the chairman has a responsibility for seeing that each member appreciates the decision that has been reached and the reasons for it. Members should never leave the retiring room in a confused state of mind and the clarification of issues and the summary of arguments is an important part of the chairman's role. The chairman will often need to check an approach to a decision with the court clerk and his colleagues. All of this can be a useful training experience for all concerned. Lay magistrates learn far more about decision making by actually reaching decisions and since they have differing experience it is important to make sure that all magistrates fully appreciate the grounds on which a decision has been reached and so develop the essential techniques of decision making. The retiring room is ideal for this purpose. Good chairmen are in a unique position to assist their colleagues.

Chapter 9

The court clerk

In the vast majority of magistrates' courts the clerk in the courtroom is not the justices' clerk but one of the justices' clerk's assistants. Regulations prescribe minimum qualifications for assistants and the regulations, when linked with the experience gained through working in court every day, are designed to ensure that lay magistrates have available to them an adequate level of legal assistance. It has long been accepted that an effective magistrates' court needs both an effective chairman and an effective and professional clerk – and for the court to be seen at its best there needs to be a good working relationship between them.

The ingredients of that relationship will inevitably be different depending upon the time, the place, the people and the case. Methods change – go in and out of fashion; local practices vary; characters and abilities count; and different cases obviously demand different handling. Since magistrates are the decision makers in their courts it is their responsibility to ensure that they get the best from their clerk. To do this the chairman of each court will need to know something about his or her clerk's personality, ability, legal expertise and skill with people. An understanding of the duties of the clerk is also helpful. It is not unreasonable to expect all these things from a lay magistrate who takes the chair in court.

More important, however, is that magistrates should understand the court clerk's legal role. The clerk's main function is to advise and assist the magistrates. He or she will have a number of other jobs to do such as dealing with the paperwork, recording decisions, assisting unrepresented parties and making a note of the proceedings, but their principal duty will always be to provide advice and assistance on matters of law to the magistrates. Decisions themselves are matters for the magistrates but an examination of the structures to be followed or subordinate decisions to be made in the course of reaching a final decision will reveal several stages at which the advice of the court clerk might be needed.

So what is the court clerk's role? In negative terms everyone knows that it is not to be party to the decisions which magistrates have to make. The much repeated description is that it is the clerk's duty to advise on "law, practice and procedure". But what does that mean apart from not being a party to the verdict or sentencing decisions? What about questions of mixed law and fact?

After much discussion about what the court clerk should *not* do following certain infamous cases heard by the High Court, the Lord Chief Justice, Lord Lane, delivered a Practice Direction ([1981] 2 All ER 831) in which he set out the majority of functions which make up the legal role of the clerk. It is well worth reproducing in full:

2 July 1981

"1. A justices' clerk is responsible to the justices for the performance of any of the functions set out below by any member of his staff acting as court clerk and may be called in to advise the justices even when he is not personally sitting with the justices as clerk to the court.

2. It shall be the responsibility of the justices' clerk to advise the justices as follows:

(a) on questions of law or of mixed law and fact;

(b) as to matters of practice and procedure.

3. If it appears to him necessary to do so, or he is so requested by the justices, the justices' clerk has the responsibility to:

(a) refresh the justices' memory as to any matter of evidence and to draw attention to any issues involved in the matters before the court;

(b) advise the justices generally on the range of

penalties which the law allows them to impose and on any guidance relevant to the choice of penalty provided by the law, the decisions of the superior courts or other authorities.

If no request for advice has been made by the justices, the justices' clerk shall discharge his responsibility in court in the presence of the parties.

4. The way in which the justices' clerk should perform his functions should be stated as follows:

    (a) The justices are entitled to the advice of their clerk when they retire in order that the clerk may fulfil his responsibility outlined above.

    (b) Some justices may prefer to take their own notes of evidence. There is, however, no obligation upon them to do so. Whether they do so or not, there is nothing to prevent them from enlisting the aid of their clerk and his notes if they are in any doubt as to the evidence which has been given.

    (c) If the justices wish to consult their clerk solely about the evidence or his notes of it, this should be done ordinarily, and certainly in simple cases, in open court. The object is to avoid any suspicion that the clerk has been involved in deciding issues of fact.

5. For the reasons stated in the Practice Direction of 15 January 1954 ([1954] 1 All ER 230) which remains in full force and effect, in domestic proceedings it is more likely than not that the justices will wish to consult their clerk. In particular, where rules of court require the reasons for their decision to be drawn up in consultation with the clerk, they will need to receive his advice for this purpose.

6. This Practice Direction is issued with the concurrence of the President of the Family Division.

Lane CJ"

Each paragraph deserves close attention.

Paragraph 1 makes it clear that the justices' clerk is

responsible for the performance of the court clerk; reminds us that the justices' clerk personally may advise or be called in to give advice even though he or she has not been present during the proceedings; and acknowledges the fact of life that in most courts the justices' clerk will not be personally present.

Paragraph 2 sets out the historical situation – now confirmed.

Paragraph 3 draws attention to the clerk's responsibilities in relation to the evidence, the issues involved in the case and the provision of advice on sentencing.

Since considerable emphasis has been placed upon the nature of the sentencing decision it is worth spending a little more time considering the clerk's role in this area. Advice upon the "range of penalties" will be needed whenever the offence is not familiar to the magistrates, and even when they are used to dealing with it they may still wish to check with their clerk before announcing certain types of sentence. "Guidance relevant to the choice of penalty provided by the law" clearly brings into play the statutory restrictions which fetter and control the discretion of magistrates, such as the need to find no other method of sentence appropriate before imposing a custodial sentence on a defendant under 21 years of age, or the requirement to call for a social enquiry report. The "decisions of superior courts or other authorities" are rarely directly available to lay magistrates and yet must have major implications for their sentencing decisions and so the court clerk must be up to date and able to pass on that guidance.

In many courts advice as to maximum penalties and ancillary matters relating to driving offences is contained in the sentencing guidelines which are provided for lay magistrates. Some benches have gone further by incorporating advice as to statutory restrictions, helpful explanations and suggestions for mode of trial decisions. Those guidelines have been drawn up by the bench and the justices' clerk working together to try to ensure that the responsibility of the clerk is fulfilled in the way the Lord Chief Justice expected. In very many cases, however, advice must relate to the facts and so the court clerk will inevitably have a major role to play in assisting the magistrates to reach their decision.

Going back to paragraph 3 it should be noted that whenever the advice to be given by the clerk has not been requested it should be given in open court in the presence of the parties. That practice has much to commend it. Professional clerks are not afraid of giving advice openly and thereby affording the lawyers and others in court the opportunity to comment upon that advice. Equally, however, lay magistrates are also entitled to receive advice from their clerk in the privacy of their retiring room and paragraph 4, which deals with the manner in which the clerk should perform his function, makes this quite clear.

Paragraph 4 also confirms the long standing practice of magistrates referring to the clerk's notes of evidence when in doubt about the evidence given – but states quite clearly that if this is the only reason for consultation with the clerk it should be done in open court.

It has always been accepted that the clerk should be the expert on law and procedure. Many may not have realised that that expertise should extend also to sentencing. Professional court clerks should be experts *on* sentencing. Magistrates should become experts *at* sentencing.

Court clerks must be professional in their approach to their work. They should be experts in their field – and given the limited area of law in which they have to specialise when compared with the solicitor in general practice, it is a proper expectation to have of them. Professional clerks will be disinterested in the cases heard by the court. They do not have to represent one side or the other and are not trying to win. Their purpose is to assist their magistrates to ensure that justice is done. Justice is their interest. Professional clerks never allow their personal beliefs, views or judgments to affect the advice which they are called upon to give.

Both lay magistrates and court clerks should feel able to seek a second opinion whenever there is uncertainty about a legal point or advice to be given. Sometimes members of benches and staff are uneasy about this – perhaps fearing damage to a close working relationship. Such fear is misguided. Professional clerks welcome second opinions and will often seek them. Today, advice given by justices' clerks is often in the form of this second opinion. With the need for efficient administrative units to support magistrates' courts the justices' clerk has to perform the role of legal consultant for a large proportion of the time.

The main point for lay magistrates to remember is that the clerk is their adviser and is there in court for them to use. That use must be a proper use – but it is suggested that if the Practice Direction is followed the result will be a court deserving of praise, not of criticism.

The following table sets out the court clerk's duties and gives examples of areas in which it is quite proper for the clerk to advise. Some would say "*should* advise". Certainly lay magistrates should consider their need for advice in each of the areas listed. The court clerk is there to be used – good magistrates will use their clerk well and to the advantage of all concerned.

Advice

It is the court clerk's duty to advise the justices on:

(a) *The law*
   As popularly understood – ingredients of offences; burden and standards of proof; the issues raised; statutory interpretation; the existence of a *prime facie* case etc.

(b) *Practice and procedure*
   Including the laws of evidence; Magistrates' Courts Rules; time limits; statutory requirements; the control of the court; assisting unrepresented parties etc.

(c) *The evidence given in the case*
   By refreshing justices' memories following referral to the court clerk's notes.

(d) *The law of sentencing*
   Including sentencing powers; the range of

penalties locally available; local decisions (for consistency); statutory controls; decisions of higher courts and authoritative advice (Home Office circulars etc.); matters consequential on conviction and sentence etc.

It is professional practice to offer as much of this advice as possible in open court.

Check List

The charge	Is an offence disclosed? Was the information in time? What kind of procedure must follow?
The defendant	Legal representation – is it necessary? Legal Aid.
Remands	If a case has to be adjourned – for how long? Does the Bail Act apply – on what grounds – are they "substantial"? What conditions can be applied?
Mode of trial	What are the statutory requirements – what advice is available from higher courts on procedure and sentencing?
The plea	Should it be accepted or is it equivocal?
The prosecution case	What are the legal elements of the offence? Can the evidence put before the court establish a case to answer? What is the burden of proof?
The evidence	What is hearsay: can it be admitted? Is it relevant? Is it prejudicial?
The defence case	What issues have been raised? What matters agreed? Does the defence have to prove anything?
Procedure	Does there have to be a set ritual? Is the witness an expert? Can the advocate "lead"? Can cross-examination really be "cross"?
The verdict	Can the clerk's notes on the evidence help? Do some legal points follow from findings of fact? Are they mixed?
The sentence	Are there any principles to be considered? What is the maximum penalty? Is there a bench norm?

What (if anything) have the higher courts said about this type of offence (offender)?

Is a social enquiry report required? Are there any statutory restrictions, eg on sending young people to prison? Should the defendant be legally represented at this stage? What alternatives are available? Should compensation be considered? What is the law on costs? Disqualifications? Endorsements and penalty points? Are reasons required or necessary?

The pronouncement Is it legally correct? Does the defendant have to agree to anything? Are the reasons sufficient? Would an explanation assist?

A final check with the clerk is always worthwhile. Nothing can be more embarrassing than the clerk having publicly to cause a correction to be made or a decision changed because of the law. Only slightly less embarrassing is the clerk having to explain the sentence or what has been said.

Appendix

Sample cases

The fictitious cases set out below may be used as exercises in implementing the Structures set out in Chapters 2 to 7.

The *Cheriton* case (see below, page 61) was originally devised by John Wagstaff, Principal Assistant Training Officer for Magistrates in Hampshire, whose co-operation is appreciated.

1. A bail application: R v Patrick Paws
[see Chapter 6]
Heard Monday 12 August 1985

Patrick Paws of 9 Freedom Villas
                 Volt Avenue
                 Portsmouth
Date of Birth: 4 April 1962
Age: 23
Unemployed
is charged that he
"On the 10 August assaulted Frederick Fox a Constable of the Hampshire Constabulary whilst in the execution of his duty."
Contrary to Section 51, Police Act 1964.

Prosecuting Solicitor: Your Worships, this is my application for this case to be adjourned. The file of papers has not yet been completed and the prosecution are not yet in a position to proceed today. You will hear that the defendant was only arrested on Saturday following an incident in the pedestrian precinct in Commercial Road. Other persons were arrested and have been bailed to appear in court in four weeks time. I ask that this defendant be remanded in custody for 7 days.

Your Worships, on Saturday afternoon this defendant along with about seven or eight others was seen in the precinct handing out leaflets. I understand they were to do with the campaign against nuclear arms and the 40th anniversary of the dropping of the atom bombs on Japan. Policemen were present in the precinct as part of their normal duties.

At about 4.15 pm a group of ten to twelve youths entered the precinct from Edinburgh Road. They may be described as 'skinheads'; one had a union jack type tattoo, another had a union jack on his jacket. As the two groups converged, words were exchanged, then there was some shouting and abusive language. Police saw a bit of a scuffle and moved in to break up the two groups. Your Worships can imagine the type of situation that might well have developed had the police not taken swift action.

PC Fox twice asked the anti nuclear campaigners to move on when he saw a girl from the back of this group throw a drinks can at the other group. He moved in to arrest her and as he took hold of her the group erupted. There was a great deal of shouting and pushing but in particular the defendant punched the officer hard in his chest. The officer was winded and almost lost his balance and his hold on the girl. Another officer arrested the defendant for the assault upon PC Fox.

Upon his arrest the defendant struggled violently and became extremely abusive. He was heard to shout 'Fascist Pigs' and once in the police van which had been called to the scene kicked the doors and tried to spit at officers.

Your Worships, the police object to bail on several grounds. I hand in a list of previous convictions, which are agreed and you will see that this defendant is well known to the courts. He is currently on bail to the Southampton Crown Court for a burglary charge. In addition he is the subject of a suspended sentence imposed at Bodmin Crown Court in 1983. The prosecution would ask you to say that there is a serious risk that this defendant would re-offend if released.

Further the defendant has no settled address; he moves

around the country and the address he has given to the court is what is commonly known as a "squat".

In addition he is charged with a serious offence and I am aware of the policy in these courts for offences of violence. This charge would I suggest attract a custodial sentence.

I leave it to your Worships to speculate as to whether the defendant would surrender to bail if granted by this court.

That is the prosecution application.

Defending Solicitor: I appear on behalf of the Defendant. I do not oppose the prosecution application for an adjournment but I do make application for bail for my client.

I would ask you to examine very closely the reasons given by the prosecution for refusing bail. I will submit that they do not amount to substantial grounds for believing than an exemption to the right to bail exists.

As far as the incident itself is concerned my client will strenuously deny the charge of assault. He also disputes the prosecution version of events on that day. The skinheads, as my friend called them, did approach my client and his friends and shouted abusive remarks. My client's group are well used to the jibes and taunts of other groups such as skinheads and punks and have learnt to ignore them, as they did on this occasion. A missile was thrown but not by my client or his friends, but by a passer-by, presumably a sympathiser. The police totally misread the situation and moved in to arrest the wrong person. Understandably the campaigners tried to bring this to the attention of the police officer but the allegation that the group "erupted" really is overstretching the position and shows that the police completely over-reacted. There may have been a little jostling within the group: they were unhappy about the arrest of the young lady but there was no pushing of police officers and certainly my client did not strike PC Fox in the manner suggested. It was a minor incident, over in a few seconds, and in any event things would have died a natural death had the police kept clear.

Turning to the previous convictions, Mr Paws was involved with drugs for a short time but since August

1983 he has turned away from this and has not been before the courts since then for drug offences. In any event the period of suspension expires at the end of this month and I would submit that it is most unlikely that the Crown Court would activate the eight months sentence or indeed any part of it. The offence before you today is of a completely different nature and is relatively minor. It is not even an offence for which the defendant could elect trial at the Crown Court.

In effect I would ask that you disregard what I would say was a technical breach of the suspended sentence.

The incident in November 1983 was also a minor matter of defacing a Land Rover belonging to a member of the hunt when my client was part of a Hunt Saboteurs group. The suspended sentence was not activated on this occasion, you will note.

If I may deal with the burglary charge in April of this year, my client is denying this charge. I can tell you that the burglary occurred at a furriers in Southampton; some fur coats were taken and ceremoniously burnt outside the shop. It appears the offence was perpetrated for moral reasons, certainly not for gain. My client is one of a number charged and his co-defendants will plead guilty. The police received descriptions of those involved at the scene and my client feels he has been charged because he was with the co-accused and has sympathy with their actions. He has denied involvement all along and the question of identity will be raised at the trial. Quite simply he says he was not present at the shop and knew nothing of the burglary.

My friend has asked you to say that Mr Paws has no settled address but he has lived at Freedom Villas since October last year. It is not a "squat" but an established commune. The property is owned by a person who has sympathy with views such as those held by my client. Rent is paid and the property is quite properly occupied. I ask you to say it is a settled address, the more so when I tell you that my client lives there with his common law wife and two children, the younger being only six weeks old. My client's wife is not in the best of health at the moment as she is suffering from post-natal depression and is in need of my client's support at this difficult time for her. Furthermore, Mr Paws starts work shortly for the Friends of the Earth organisation and will be involved in the collection of waste paper for recycling.

Finally I would ask you to note that whilst my client has appeared in Court on several occasions, not once has he failed to surrender to bail. Leaving aside the minor incident in November 1983 he has been out of trouble for nearly two years. The outstanding matters against him are denied, but he is settled in this area and is soon to start work. His wife desperately needs his support right now. If you grant him bail he would be willing to comply with any conditions of residence or reporting you may wish to impose.

He asks you to say that the police have not convinced you that exemptions to the right to bail exist and that a remand in custody cannot be justified.

That is my application.

Previous convictions:

4.9.81	Leicester M.C.	Possession Cannabis	Fined £35.00 Costs £10.00
12.12.81	Brighton M.C.	1 Possession Cannabis 2 Obstruct Police	1 Fined £50.00 2 Fined £50.00 Costs £20.00
30.8.83	Bodmin C.C.	1 Possession Cannabis with intent to supply 2 Cultivation Cannabis 3 Possession Class A drug (LSD)	1 6 months imprisonment 2 6 months concurrent 3 2 months consecutive All susp. for two years
4.11.83	Penzance M.C.	Criminal Damage	Fined £75.00. (No action re: Susp. Sentence)
30.4.85	Burglary	Committed to Southampton Crown Court for trial.	

The bench retires to consider whether or not to grant bail.

2. Mode of trial proceedings:
Police v Arthur Brick [See Chapter 7]

Mr Brick appears before you on summons for an offence of assaulting Doreen Brick occasioning her actual bodily harm, contrary to section 47 Offences Against the Person Act (1861). The offence took place some two months ago and Mr Brick is represented by Miss Smiley. The prosecution are represented by Mr Hurd.

Your court clerk asks Mr Hurd for his representations as to where the case can better be heard. Mr Hurd tells you that in the prosecution's opinion, the case is eminently suitable for summary trial. The short facts of the case are that Mr and Mrs Brick had been out together for the evening and were returning home by taxi in the early hours of the morning. An argument had ensued over who would pay for the taxi which had culminated in Mr Brick hitting Mrs Brick full in the face with this clenched fist. The taxi driver had then stopped to sort the trouble out and Mr Brick had run off. Because of Mrs Brick's injuries an ambulance had to be called and she was conveyed to Queen Alexandra hospital. There she was diagnosed as having a dislocated jaw, a broken nose, a chipped front tooth and two lacerations which required a total of twenty-three stitches.

In the meantime the police had been called to the scene and after the ambulance had taken Mrs Brick away, the defendant approached PC Pace and said, "It's all right mate, it was me what done it, I hope she's all right". PC Pace arrested the defendant and he was later interviewed and then released. Mrs Brick was detained overnight in hospital and allowed to return home next morning. The prosecutor concludes by opining that your powers of punishment of six months imprisonment and/or a fine of £2000 are more than adequate in this case.

For the defendant, Miss Smiley agrees that the case is suitable for summary trial. Her client, who has never been in trouble with the police before, has been unemployed for some five months after being made redundant by the engineering firm he had worked for for 16 years since leaving school. The couple live in a small one bedroomed flat and Mr Brick's unemployment has been a cause of conflict for the couple as Mrs Brick had not thought Mr Brick to be doing much to alleviate the situation. On the night in question both had had too much to drink and Mrs Brick's constant nagging on the subject had caused Mr Brick to snap and lash out at his wife. He had immediately regretted doing so and had run off more in shame than fear. On regaining his senses he had immediately given himself up to the police. After his release the couple had been living apart, but were now well on the way to patching things up and there was a possibility of a reconciliation. Mr Brick was now again in full-time employment and the root cause of the trouble was no longer present.

No weapon had been used in the assault – the cuts having been caused by a large ring on Mr Brick's index finger – and Mrs Brick had not suffered any long term injury as a result of the one punch.

All in all, concludes Miss Smiley, this was an isolated incident of the sort dealt with by magistrates' courts regularly and she sees no reason why this matter should go to the Crown Court.

The bench retires to consider which court should hear this case.

3. Application for an adjournment: Police v Julia Anne Cheriton
[See Chapter 5]

Court clerk: This case first came before the court sixteen weeks ago when Mrs Cheriton appeared in answer to a summons. The case was then adjourned four weeks for her to see a solicitor.

Twelve weeks ago, Mrs Cheriton's solicitor, Mr Hawkley, requested advance disclosure of the prosecution case and a further adjournment of four weeks was allowed. Then eight weeks ago, having consented to be tried summarily, Mrs Cheriton entered a not guilty plea and because of holiday problems with the witnesses the case was adjourned to today and a morning set aside for it to be heard.

I am told, however, that Mr Densmead, for the prosecution, has an application to make.

Mr Densmead: Your Worships – I apply for an adjournment of the case because one of my witnesses, the officer in the case, PC Warnford, is on leave and is not available today. Also, Mr Blackfield, the manager of the store involved in this case of shoplifting is not yet at court. My friend, Mr Hawkley for the defence, has no objections to this application.

Court clerk: Why has the officer been allowed to go on leave when this case was listed for hearing eight weeks ago – weren't his leave dates known then – and why isn't Mr Blackmore here?

Mr Densmead: I'm afraid there has been a bit of a mix up in the prosecution office over this case and it wasn't until yesterday that I discovered that the witnesses had not been warned. Mr Blackfield and Miss Hound have been contacted this morning. Miss Hound is here and I'm told that Mr Blackfield is on his way.

Looking at my file it is clear that the officer had not disclosed his leave dates when the case was adjourned. We do normally try to avoid an officer's leave dates.

Mr Hawkley: If it would help your Worships – I do not oppose my friend's application. Indeed it would assist me. I have two other cases to deal with this morning – one in the juvenile court – and I am afraid there is no-one else in my office who can help. Also I have not taken full instructions yet.

Court Clerk: Mr Hawkley – would you please explain to the court why you have not received full instructions yet.

Mr Hawkley: Mrs Cheriton had an appointment to see me two days ago but unfortunately she did not attend – I think there must have been problems at home or something. Be that as it may I have not had the opportunity to take full instructions.

The Court retires to make a decision.

4. Submission of no case to answer: Police v Julia Anne Cheriton

[see Chapter 4]

Defendant:	Mrs Julia Anne CHERITON (27)
Charge:	On 9 September at Basingport in Hampshire stole a packet of Cadbury's chocolate buttons value 14p the property of Minimart Ltd, contrary to s 1(1) Theft Act 1968.
Prosecuting solicitor:	Mr Densmead
Defence solicitor:	Mr Hawkley
Mode of trial:	Both parties ask for summary trial; justices agree.
Plea:	Defendant consents to summary trial; Not guilty.

Mr Densmead opens the prosecution's case:

The allegation is that Mrs Cheriton was shopping at Minimart on a Thursday morning. She was waiting in the queue for the check-out with a full shopping trolley and her 18 months old child standing beside her. The child was seen to take a packet of chocolate buttons from the display and proceed to eat them. Mrs Cheriton could not have failed to see what the child was doing. Nevertheless, she did not draw the fact to the attention of the till assistant, and made no attempt to pay for the buttons. When interviewed she admitted that she knew exactly what was going on and said she never intended to pay for the sweets.

Prosecution witnesses

Shirley Hound (18) sworn:
I am a till operator at Minimart Ltd. On Thursday 9 September I was on duty at till 4 in the store. We were very busy that morning. I recall Mrs Cheriton because of what I was told afterwards. At the time I was dealing with her I did not notice that she had a child with her. I was too busy. If I had seen the child with some chocolate buttons I would have demanded payment for them.

Cross-examined by Mr Hawkley:

The confectionery display is sited on both sides of each till, forming a short corridor along which the queue forms. Sweets of various sorts are on display in open shelves from six inches above the ground to about shoulder height. There is nothing to stop people taking the items from the shelves. That is the idea of self-service shops. Children often take sweets from the display at the tills. They sometimes shout and shout until their mothers agree to buy the sweets. There are no sweets anywhere else in the store.

I have worked on refilling the confectionery shelves. I agree that it is inconvenient to fill the lower ones because of the restricted space and the bending involved. I don't know why the store puts them there. I've never thought about it. All the shops do it.

Martin Graham Blackfield (32) sworn:

I am the Deputy Manager of Minimart Ltd. On Thursday, 9 September I was on duty supervising the operation of the tills. I noticed Mrs Cheriton waiting in the till queue with her trolley and her child. The little boy was standing on the ground beside her in the approach to the tills. As I watched he took a packet of chocolate buttons worth 14p from the confectionery display. He tore the packet open, dropping a few buttons on the floor, and began to eat the chocolate.

When the queue moved forwards Mrs Cheriton bent down to speak to the boy. She must have noticed that he was holding the packet. She moved him forward, and Miss Hound began to deal with her purchases. When the trolley was half empty, Mrs Cheriton bent down again and picked up her son. She lifted him onto the child seat in the trolley. He was still holding the buttons, and by now his fingers and mouth were covered with melted chocolate.

I was expecting Mrs Cheriton to point out the buttons to Miss Hound and pay for them, but she said nothing. The check-out was completed and Mrs Cheriton paid for the items in the trolley, coming to £35.16. Then she pushed the trolley, with the child in it, beyond the till into the loading area, and put the shopping back in the trolley. All this time the child was sitting facing her only a few inches from her face. She paused, took out her handkerchief, and wiped the chocolate from the child's mouth. Then she pushed the trolley out of the exit towards the car park.

I stopped her and told her that I thought she had something she had not paid for. I asked her to return to the shop with me. She refused. She told me to check the till roll against the items in her trolley. I said that it was the buttons in the little boy's hand that I was talking about. She said "Well, I didn't take those, did I? I don't approve of sweets." I asked her again to come back to the shop so that we could talk about it. She said she was in a hurry, but she gave me a card with her name and address on it. Rather than cause her any embarrassment by making an arrest I allowed her to go, but I told her that I would be contacting the police.

I later telephoned the police station and told PC Warnford what I had seen.

Cross-examined by Mr Hawkley:

I agree with Shirley Hound's description of the confectionery display. The purpose of these shelves being where they are is to attract the attention of shoppers while they are waiting at the check-out. Sweets are not something that people tend to put on their shopping lists, so you need to remind them about them, and the best way to do that is to put them where they will have to stare at them while they wait for the tills.

The bottom shelf of this display is no lower than the bottom shelves in other parts of the shop; they are standard units. I agree that children sometimes nag their parents for sweets from these shelves. I would not agree that we are cashing in on the pressure children can exert on their parents in a crowded shop. I would not agree with the word "exploitation". I think this is a legitimate trading practice.

Mrs Cheriton's manner was polite and cheerful. She did

not seem in any way surprised or distraught. She simply took the attitude that it was nothing to do with her.

It surprises me to learn that Mrs Cheriton's child is a girl. I thought it was a boy. It was wearing dungarees and a blue jumper, so I suppose I jumped to a conclusion.

PC 5885 Nigel Warnford sworn:

On Friday, 10 September as a result of a complaint from Mr Blackfield I visited the defendant at her home address. I cautioned her and the following conversation took place.

Q   I am investigating a complaint about a theft from Minimart yesterday.

A   Oh yes. You mean when Cathy took the buttons. She's asleep just now, but I'll wake her up if you want to interrogate her. I thought children under ten were incapable of committing a criminal offence, though.

Q   You were with her yesterday, weren't you?

A   Yes, of course.

Q   What happened?

A   She took some buttons from those stupid shelves near the till and ate them.

Q   Did you see her do it?

A   No.

Q   When did you realise she'd done it?

A   When she opened the packet.

Q   Why didn't you stop her?

A   If the shop doesn't want children to eat their property they should keep the tempting items out of reach. It's not for me to look after their goods for them.

Q   But you're responsible for your child?

A   They can sue me in the County Court if they think so, and it'll be up to the Registrar to decide how far their negligence contributed to what happened.

Q   How old is Cathy?

A   Eighteen months.

Q   So you saw your baby daughter eating sweets that you knew she wasn't entitled to?

A   Yes
Q   Did you tell the check-out girl about them?
A   No
Q   Why not?
A   I think I've answered that already.
Q   You never had any intention of paying for the chocolate, did you?
A   Absolutely not.

I cautioned her again, and told her she would be reported for consideration of the question of prosecuting her for theft. She made no reply.

No cross-examination.

Close of prosecution case.

Mr Hawkley makes a submission for the defence:

Your worships, there is no dispute about the facts of this case. We do not suggest that the witnesses are telling anything but the absolute truth.

However, I do wish to submit that there is no case for Mrs Cheriton to answer on the charge of theft.

No-one suggests that Mrs Cheriton herself took the buttons. Equally no-one denies that Mrs Cheriton knew about Cathy taking them. The prosecution case rests on the notion that Mrs Cheriton was somehow responsible through her daughter for the taking of the sweets. No doubt in ordinary language that is correct. Most people will accept that they are responsible for the actions of their babies. That is precisely the psychological point which the store depends upon when it sets up this special form of high-pressure salesmanship. They expect children to take things; they expect parents to feel guilty and pay for them.

Perhaps, in civil law, that is legally correct (though I am far from convinced of it). But we are not dealing with civil law. This is a criminal charge, taken from section 1 of the Theft Act. The Theft Act makes it quite clear what theft consists of. I don't need to remind this bench of the definition. Suffice it to say that it clearly contemplates

65

one person taking a direct, positive, action of their own volition. Has Mrs Cheriton "appropriated" the buttons? Surely not, not in any ordinary meaning of that word.

It may be that the prosecution might have succeeded if they had proceeded with a charge of aiding and abetting theft. That is another matter. They chose to charge the substantive offence of theft, and for this there is no legal basis. I invite you to dismiss the case.

Mr Densmead replies for the prosecution:
There are no authorities I can cite directly bearing on this issue. I would only ask the bench to use its commonsense and say that a child of 18 months is so manifestly dependent on its parent and the parent is so completely responsible for the child, that the child's actions become one in law with those of its parent. To decide otherwise would be to give carte blanche to a whole new area of shoplifting with impunity.

I ask you to reject the submission.

The court clerk advises the justices in open court that there are no legal authorities on either side of the argument, and it is up to the bench to decide which of the views propounded by the advocates is to be preferred as a matter of legal and public policy.

The court retires to consider the submission.

5. A verdict decision — guilty or not guilty: Police v Julia Anne Cheriton

[See Chapter 2]
Proceed on the basis that in sample case 4 it has been decided that there is a case to answer and now consider the case for the defence:

Mr Hawkley says that he has only one witness to call — his client Mrs Cheriton:

Mrs Julia Anne Cheriton (27) sworn:

I live at Flat 19, Whitchurch House, Andover Way, Basingport with my three children.

I did go shopping in the Minimarket on 9 September and a lot of what the shop assistant and the store manager have said is true. It is quite true that I did discover that Cathy had taken some chocolate buttons – she must have taken them from the display next to the till.

As far as I am concerned Cathy had taken the buttons. I was not responsible for that. In any case she had eaten them before I could do anything about it. I did not intend to steal the chocolate buttons – I had no reason to believe Cathy would take them – she wouldn't have done if the shop had not put them on display right next to the till – deliberately to tempt children. I thought it was the shop's own fault and didn't see why I should pay – but I certainly didn't think I was being dishonest. I refused to pay on a point of principle – not dishonesty.

Cross-examined by Mr Densmead:

Yes – I do know what dishonesty means. I have told the truth. I was not trying to get away with anything.

If I had not been stopped I don't suppose I would have said anything to anyone.

I can't remember whether I noticed that Cathy had the buttons before or after I had gone through the check-out. It was probably afterwards.

No, I don't think I should be responsible for my daughter's actions. She does have a mind of her own, you know. It was the shop's fault anyway. They deserve to lose the sweets they display to exploit children.

I did not offer to pay for the buttons. I did not intend to pay. I didn't think I had to.

I don't think it was my duty to tell the check-out girl.

I suppose I was being awkward – but it was the shop's fault.

Yes, I did say that Cathy was not old enough to commit a crime. Yes, I did know that Cathy was eating the buttons. I suppose it might have been before I paid for the other goods.

No! I was not trying to get away with it. It was a matter of principle.

I didn't bring the buttons to the cashier's attention because it was their fault — they should pay for trying to tempt children with sweets. It serves them right that Cathy ate the buttons.

No re-examination

Mr Hawkley on behalf of the defendant then addresses the Bench:
Your Worships — I think that I have already made the points I would wish to put before you when I submitted that there was no case to answer. I still hold to that view. With respect, it is quite clear that Mrs Cheriton is not guilty of theft. The prosecution have not proved their case and in any event any doubt has to be resolved in favour of my client and so she must be acquitted. I do not think that I need say any more.

The Court retires to reach a verdict.

6. A sentence decision: Police v Julia Anne Cheriton

[See Chapter 3]
Proceed on the basis that Mrs Cheriton has been found guilty. Mr Hawkley does not wish to make a mitigating address but simply asks the court to read the following social enquiry report:

SOCIAL ENQUIRY REPORT

on

Mrs Julia Anne CHERITON

Appearing at:	Basingport Magistrates' Ct	on:	
Address:	Flat 19, Whitchurch House	Age: 27	DOB:
	Andover Way, Basingport	Status:	Separated
PSD:	Basingport	Occupation:	
Charge:	Theft of chocolate buttons		

1. Mrs Cheriton is a married woman, separated from her husband. She occupies a council flat on the Chelford Wood Estate and has responsibility for three children, aged 10 years, 5 years and 20 months. Her oldest child is the result of a relationship with a married man when she was a teenager. She married Mr Cheriton, an electronics engineer, when she was 21 and appears to have had a normal happy relationship until the birth of their second child, some 18 months ago. It was a difficult pregnancy, with frequent visits to hospital and it was during this period that her husband formed a relationship with a secretary at the firm for which he works and left home. I understand that it is his intention to seek a divorce and marry this woman. Mr Cheriton regularly visits his children.

2. Mrs Cheriton is an intelligent, articulate woman, somewhat embittered by her disappointing relationships and with a hostile attitude to authority. An only child, her parents separated when she was 15 years old and although she did well at school (7 'O' levels) she did not continue her education beyond the secondary stage. That period was particularly difficult for her as both parents had formed associations with partners and moved away from the area. She did not find it easy to settle with either parent and ran away from "home", committing a series of offences whilst on the run. Eventually she was made the subject of a care order and after short periods in various children's homes was placed with foster parents with whom she seemed to settle – sufficiently to complete her education and, through the efforts of her foster father, obtain a job with a firm of solicitors. Despite her record she seemed to have a promising secretarial career in front of her when she formed an association with a member of that firm and had to leave. By then she was pregnant and the relationship was terminated. She returned to the neighbourhood in which she had been brought up and shortly before the birth of her first child was convicted of her first offence as an adult – theft from Minimart Limited.

3. Although she was made the subject of a one year probation order which she successfully completed, it is obvious that she feels bitter about this episode in her life and argues that she had been left almost destitute and was justified in stealing in order to feed herself and the baby she was expecting. Our records show that her supervising officer never felt close to Mrs Cheriton and was unable to discuss personal issues with her.

4. She eventually met Mr Cheriton, a young engineer and they married and her second child was born soon after. It appears to have been a good marriage for the first three or four years but difficulties in their personal relationship led to many arguments and a quite rapid deterioration. Her husband says that he would have left home earlier but was worried about his wife and tried to see her through the pregnancy. Unfortunately, he found Julia to be "difficult and unpredictable" and unable to establish the stable, mature relationship that he wanted. I believe he is fond of all three children. He tries to visit them as often as he can.

5. When Mr Cheriton left home, Mrs Cheriton provided accommodation for "a lodger". Unfortunately she did not disclose this information to the DHSS, nor is she frank as to the nature of that relationship. She was eventually prosecuted, fined and ordered to repay the Department. She still owes well over £300 to the court. She deeply resents the way she was handled, particularly because certain information was obtained from the neighbours with whom she no longer communicates.

6. Nine months ago, she appeared before the Newbury Court following an incident at one of the Greenham Common Peace Women's Camps and was bound over to keep the peace for 12 months in the sum of £50. That order still stands.

7. Her attitude to the present offence is clear and she refuses to accept any responsibility. She says that unknown to her the sweets were taken by her 18

month old daughter from a low display shelf. She feels that it was unreasonable to expect her to watch her child's every action and in any case the value of the articles was negligible. She suspects that the manager of the Minimart is hostile to her and that he would not have taken action with any other customer.

8. It is not easy to come to any clear recommendation in this case. Mrs Cheriton gives the impression of being a competent, independent woman who despite straightened circumstances manages quite well. Her three bedroomed flat is clean and comfortable, although sparsely furnished, and her children seem well cared for. There is certainly a strong bond of affection between them. Unfortunately, she has very few friends and a hostile atmosphere remains between her and her neighbours. She has no contact with her parents who have both established their own families away from the area. She deeply resents interference in her private affairs and although she co-operated with the preparation of this report she would not agree to a further period of probation. She has very modest means and the large amount of fines and compensation still outstanding make a financial penalty inappropriate. When discussing the possible outcome of the case she maliciously pointed out that she could be imprisoned for the offence and that local publicity would bring discredit on the courts, the police and the shop involved. Although this is her sixth court appearance I would suggest that this is a very different offence from the others and that despite her anti-social attitude the court may feel a discharge an appropriate way of dealing with it.

S H Jesturr
Senior Probation Officer

Antecedents

1. *Full name*: Mrs Julia Anne Cheriton
2. *Address*: Flat 19, Whitchurch House, Andover Way, Basingport

3. *Age*: 27
4. *Place of birth*: Basingport
5. *Nationality*: British
6. *Status*: ~~Single~~/~~Married~~/Separated/~~Divorced~~/~~Widowed~~
7. *Education*: Attended school at Basingport Grammar School for Girls, leaving at 16
8. *Home conditions, domestic circumstances and financial commitments*: Married with three children – but separated from her husband. In receipt of DHSS Supplementary Benefit and Family Allowance for the children.
9. *Main Employments*: Has had several secretarial/clerical jobs. Not worked for the past six years.
10. *Outstanding matters*: Subject of a bind over at Newbury Magistrates' Court
11. *Previous Convictions*

COURT	OFFENCE	SENTENCE
Basingport Juv Ct	Breaking and entering 4 offences (6 TICs)	Care Order
Basingport Juv Ct	Theft from shop 2 offences	Fined £20
Basingport Mag Ct	Theft from shop	Probation One year
Basingport Mag Ct	DHSS Fraud 3 offences (32 TICs)	Fined £150 Compensation £350
Newbury Mag Ct	Breach of the Peace	Bound over in sum of £100 for 12 months

The court retires to decide upon sentence.